R.L. Stine

by Julie Murray

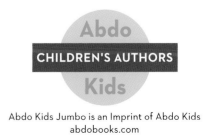

CHILDREN'S AUTHORS

Abdo Kids Jumbo is an Imprint of Abdo Kids
abdobooks.com

abdobooks.com

Published by Abdo Kids, a division of ABDO, P.O. Box 398166, Minneapolis, Minnesota 55439.
Copyright © 2022 by Abdo Consulting Group, Inc. International copyrights reserved in all countries.
No part of this book may be reproduced in any form without written permission from the publisher.
Abdo Kids Jumbo™ is a trademark and logo of Abdo Kids.

Printed in the United States of America, North Mankato, Minnesota.

102021

012022

Photo Credits: Alamy, Getty Images, iStock, Seth Poppel/Yearbook Library, Shutterstock PREMIER,
©Jasperdo p7 / CC BY-NC-ND 2.0, ©VCU Libraries p7 / CC BY-NC 2.0, ©Sundial Magazine p9, /
CC-BY-SA 3.0, ©alain l.e. p13 / CC BY-NC-ND 2.0, ©Goosebumps Wiki p15 / CC-BY-SA 3.0

Production Contributors: Teddy Borth, Jennie Forsberg, Grace Hansen
Design Contributors: Candice Keimig, Pakou Moua

Library of Congress Control Number: 2020948017
Publisher's Cataloging-in-Publication Data

Names: Murray, Julie, author.

Title: R.L. Stine / by Julie Murray

Description: Minneapolis, Minnesota : Abdo Kids, 2022 | Series: Children's authors | Includes online
    resources and index.

Identifiers: ISBN 9781098207250 (lib. bdg.) | ISBN 9781098208097 (ebook) | ISBN 9781098208516
    (Read-to-Me ebook)

Subjects: LCSH: Stine, R. L. (Robert Lawrence) --Juvenile literature. | Authors--Biography--Juvenile
    literature. | Children's books--Juvenile literature.

Classification: DDC 809.8928--dc23

Table of Contents

Early Years

Robert Lawrence Stine was born on October 8, 1943, in Columbus, Ohio.

Columbus, Ohio

Bob enjoyed telling stories and reading. He especially liked funny comics like *Mad* magazine and scary comics like *Tales from the Crypt*.

Bob started writing at an early age. He wrote jokes and funny stories using a typewriter. In college, he wrote for *Sundial*, the school's **humor magazine**.

SUNDIAL
The Zoo Around Us

25c

ALL NEW SICKENING FORMAT!
Appalling Conclusion:
THE LAST ANGRY WEREWOLF

Special:
MEET THE EXCITING SINGING
GROUP FROM ENGLAND!

After college, Bob moved to New York City, New York. He got a job writing. He helped create two **humor magazines** called *Maniacs* and *Bananas*. He also wrote his first book, *How to be Funny*.

Scary Books

In 1986, Stine's first scary book, *Blind Date*, was published. It was a big success! Its popularity led to the Fear Street series.

13

Stine decided to write scary books for a younger audience. In 1992, he published his first Goosebumps book. It was called *Welcome to Dead House*.

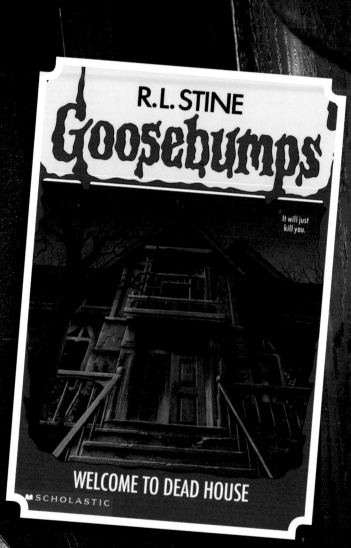

Goosebumps grabbed the attention of many readers. The original **series** had 62 books. Many **spin-offs** followed. It was even made into a TV show and movies!

Stine created other popular book series including Rotten School and Just Beyond.

Legacy

Whether scary or funny in genre, Stine's books keep his audience reading. More than 400 million book copies have sold worldwide! Stine continues to write books for kids from his home in New York City.

Timeline

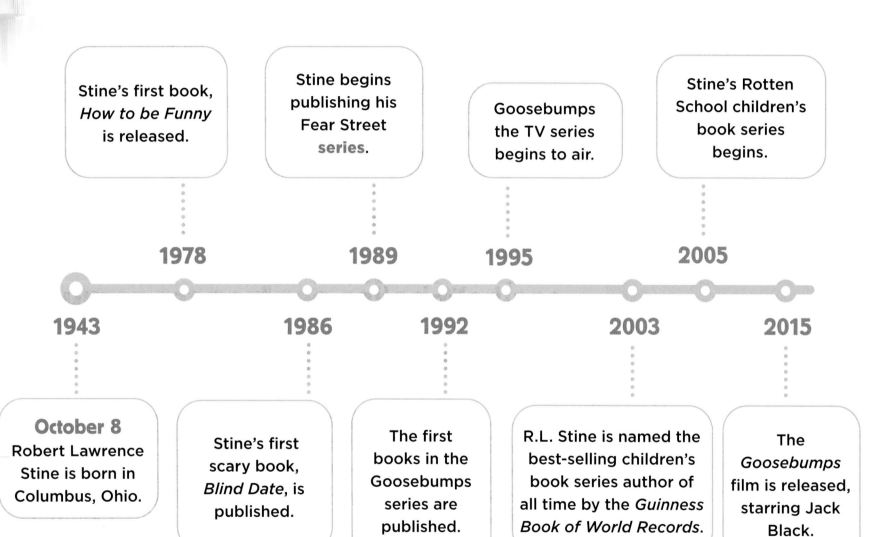

Stine's first book, *How to be Funny* is released.

Stine begins publishing his Fear Street series.

Goosebumps the TV series begins to air.

Stine's Rotten School children's book series begins.

1978

1989

1995

2005

1943

1986

1992

2003

2015

October 8 Robert Lawrence Stine is born in Columbus, Ohio.

Stine's first scary book, *Blind Date*, is published.

The first books in the Goosebumps series are published.

R.L. Stine is named the best-selling children's book series author of all time by the *Guinness Book of World Records*.

The *Goosebumps* film is released, starring Jack Black.

Glossary

genre – a particular type, sort, or category.

humor magazine – a magazine designed to provide funny content for its readers.

series – a group of related things that come one after another.

spin-off – in media, something newly created that focuses on more details and different aspects of an original work.

23

Index

Abdo Kids ONLINE
FREE! ONLINE MULTIMEDIA RESOURCES

Visit **abdokids.com** to access crafts, games, videos, and more!

Use Abdo Kids code **CRK7250** or scan this QR code!